C000009946

THE COUNTY DURHAM BOOK

3rd Edition

1st Edition 1973
2nd Edition 1981
3rd Edition 1992

Cover Photograph: *Durham Cathedral and Castle, from Flass Vale.*

1. (opposite): *Hamsterley Forest at dawn.*

Designed and Published by The British Publishing Company Ltd, Gloucester for Durham County Council

Printed and bound by White Crescent Press, Luton on environmentally friendly paper

Copyright © Durham County Council

Hardback: ISBN 07140 2965 3

Paperback: ISBN 07140 2966 1

Photography by Philip Nixon

Edited by Martin Kay, designed by Karen Rankin.

DURHAM
COUNTY
COUNCIL

A FIRST CLASS COUNTY

THE COUNTY DURHAM BOOK

2. County Durham in the early 17th Century.

Foreword

The 'County Durham Book' is essentially a photographic portrayal of life in the Land of the Prince Bishops. It traces the history of the County through the centuries from pre-Roman times to the present day.

The book encapsulates the quality of life in this richly diverse County – the castles and historic houses, the delightful dales villages, the lovely countryside and open moors and the magnificent Norman Cathedral in the City of Durham. Furthermore it demonstrates what the County is like as a place in which to live and work and it shows what has been done to tackle the restructuring of the economy following the decline of the County's traditional industries.

County Durham has an inherent sense of identity and continuity which goes back hundreds of years. The County's long tradition and heritage is reflected in its residents' deep rooted sense of belonging to County Durham. Through building on the strength of this tradition, the people of the County have the confidence and ability to adapt, to change and meet the challenges of the 21st Century.

I am proud of County Durham and all it has to offer and am very pleased to have this opportunity, as Chairman of the County Council, to be able to contribute this foreword to such a high quality and enjoyable publication.

G. W. Terrans

CHAIRMAN
DURHAM COUNTY
COUNCIL

List of Illustrations

Reference numbers refer to the map grid on page 102.

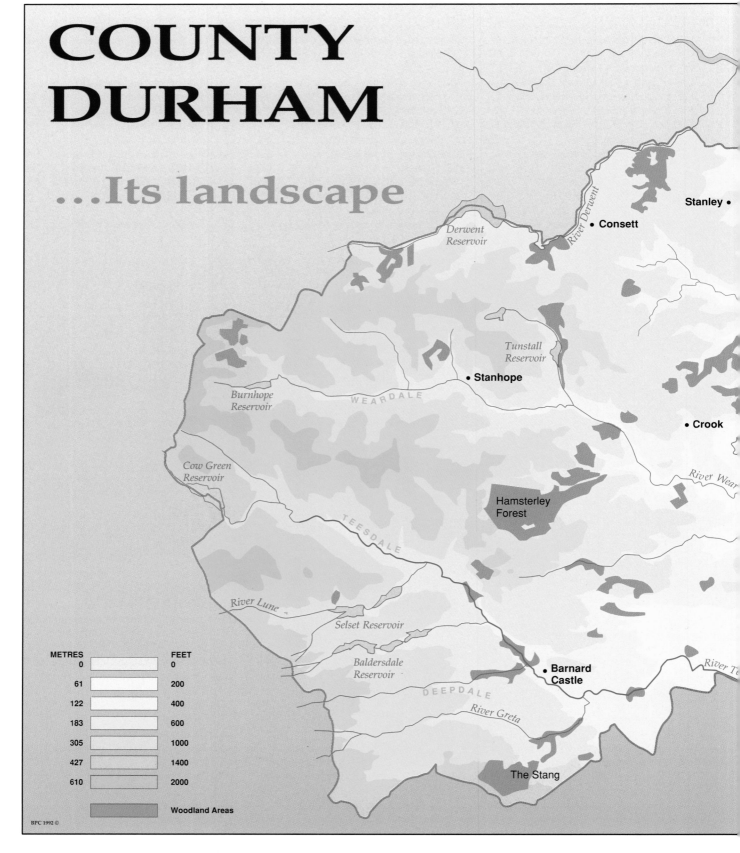

COUNTY DURHAM

...Its landscape

Stanley •

Derwent
Reservoir

River Derwent

• Consett

Tunstall
Reservoir

• Stanhope

WEARDALE

• Crook

Burnhope
Reservoir

Cow Green
Reservoir

River Wear

Hamsterley
Forest

TEESDALE

River Lune

Selset Reservoir

METRES		FEET
0		0
61		200
122		400
183		600
305		1000
427		1400
610		2000

Woodland Areas

Baldersdale
Reservoir

• Barnard
Castle

River Te

DEEPDALE

River Greta

The Stang

BPC 1992 ©

8

Contents

3. Left: County Durham ... Its landscape.

THE COUNTY DURHAM BOOK

Introduction

4. (above) Langdon Beck village with Cronkley Scar in the background.

On the North Sea coast, stretching high into the Pennines, lies a pearl of history, heritage and countryside. County Durham is rich in each. Its contribution to the nation is remarkable. Its attraction as a place in which to live and grow is considerable. We believe this book will help both residents and visitors alike to appreciate it fully.

County Durham's place in the geography of the north east is easy to understand. It lies between the populated areas of Tyneside to the north and Teeside to the south. In contrast to built up areas of Newcastle, Gateshead and Sunderland on the one hand, and Middlesbrough on the other, County Durham is essentially rural. Its freshness and green open spaces are cherished as much by urban visitors as by those who have made their home here.

The County's recorded history extends back over 1,000 years - an extraordinary adventure through time which is there to be enjoyed today. Whether one's taste is for medieval or more recent social history, there is much to discover and reflect upon in the castles and communities of County Durham. Even high up in the glorious dales, where there is cottage industry, there remains compelling evidence of yesterday's harsh existence.

Much has changed over the years, not least the boundaries of the County itself. However the Blaydon Races, the Jarrow March and the Stockton and Darlington Railway remain firmly part of popular tradition for County Durham. However much coal mining may be fading from the local economy, pride and strong memories remain there too.

County Durham has many striking contrasts and yet there is a cohesiveness about its constituent parts. Enterprise, opportunity and optimism flourish in this place. The tradition of the Land of the Prince Bishops undoubtedly lives on.

Landscape

5. *(above) The view from Langdon Common across the dale where the River Tees has cut a deep valley between Cronkley and Widdybank Fells.*

6. *(left) High Force, River Tees.*

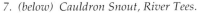

7. *(below) Cauldron Snout, River Tees.*

County Durham is mainly rural with strong contrasts in the character of the countryside. Its 1,000 square miles (2,500 square kilometres) rise from low wooded valleys along the North Sea coast, through ridges and rolling farmland, to the upper moors of the Pennines themselves. There is much charm here - but much raw beauty, too.

In the far west, at 2,600 feet (790 metres) above sea level, Mickle Fell dominates the Lunedale landscape. The limestone of these furthest hills was laid down in shallow seas over 300 million years ago. That which is found around Frosterley contains many fossils and has been prized as an ornamental building stone since the earliest days.

Punctuating the limestone are huge slabs, or 'sills', of dolerite. A magnificent example is the Great Whin Sill at well-named High Force, where the torrent of peat brown water plunging in spate is truly awe-inspiring.

8. (right) Widdybank Fell.

9. (below) Cronkley Scar – a huge outcrop of quartz dolerite, an igneous rock which penetrated the Carboniferous Limestone of the area nearly 300 million years ago.

The dolerite was formed at depth and later revealed by earth movements. In places, the intense heat baked the surface limestone into harder marble. In Upper Teesdale, for example, the process produced 'sugar limestones' upon which grow rare Arctic and Alpine plants. Over a period of time, water flowing through these rocks absorbed their chemical traces and combined with the surrounding limestone to form deposits of vein minerals such as lead and fluorspar.

Further to the east, where thick bands of sandstone have formed over the limestone, peat and heather-clad moors stretch for mile upon mile. The air is fresh and invigorating. One can walk freely and in perfect solitude. Only the sheep and grouse intrude.

10. (left) Fossilised Tree at Stanhope in Weardale.

11. (below) A fluorspar mine at Wolfcleugh Common in Weardale – fluorspar was a then useless by-product of the days of lead mining but has several modern applications.

12. *(above) Inhabitant of the upland moors – the curlew.*

13. *(below) Inhabitant of the upland moors – the red grouse.*

14. (above) Sedling Rake drovers' road, Weardale.

15. (below) Sheep on the moors at Muggleswick.

16. *(above left)* *Mountain Pansies.*

17. *(left)* *Pyrenean Lily – this unusual example grows on the edge of Hamsterley Forest.*

18. *(above)* *Spotted Orchids.*

19. *(right)* *Spring Gentian grows only in the special conditions of Teesdale in England above 1,200 feet – it flowers from April to June.*

20. (above) Heather on Knitsley Fell.

21. (below) The Derwent Valley.

22. (right) The River Derwent.

County Durham's three beautiful rivers rise with their tributaries among these western hills. To the south, the Tees gushes over some of England's most impressive waterfalls before leaving the County below the market town of Darlington. To the north, the Derwent flows past upland deciduous and conifer woods to join eventually with the Tyne. In the centre, the Wear descends to curl proudly around the roots of Durham's cathedral and bathe the ruins of Finchale Priory.

As with the Tees and the Derwent, the lowest stretches of the Wear are also now outside the County. However, the character of the rivers is undeniably that of the Durham Dales where each has cut spectacularly into the moors.

23. (left) Witton Bridge, Witton le Wear – an interesting example of an old coaching bridge.

24. (above) Framwellgate Bridge over the River Wear at Durham City was originally built in the 12th Century – the gateway was later removed in order that the roadway might be widened.

25. (right) Low Force on the River Tees is possibly the prettiest waterfall in County Durham – many rare and beautiful flowers flourish on its banks.

26. (above) The Wynch Bridge at Bowlees, River Tees – constructed in 1704, the original bridge was reputedly the first suspension bridge in England. It was reconstructed around 1830 following a fire.

27. (below) The view over Teesdale from Whistle Crag is well-known in County Durham – from this high vantage point the differences between the seasons are particularly well displayed.

Great reservoirs can be found among the upland valleys, some deep in meditation, others bright blue jewels. The neat pastureland along their sides and down the dales themselves is patterned by stone walls and stone-built farms and cottages.

In picturesque Teesdale, many of the buildings are carefully whitewashed, as if a landscaper planned this charming valley. In lovely Weardale, the ambience seems original, almost primitive in comparison. Around the River Derwent, the views are more open and the treasures lie hidden in wooded hollows.

Whatever may distinguish them, the Durham Dales and all that lies around them rightly form part of an Area of Outstanding Natural Beauty. Snow stays long upon the upper slopes. Small towns and villages shelter snugly along the valley bottoms. Daffodils everywhere brighten the village greens in spring. The autumn colours of the many trees complete a striking, changing backcloth.

28. (top) Snow in Upper Weardale.

29. (above) Snow at Cowshill in Weardale.

30. (below) Derwent Reservoir.

31. (left) At the edge of Muggleswick Common near Middles Farm, Waskerley Sike, a tributary of Hisehope Burn has cut a deep valley into the moorland.

32. (right) Leicester Sheep in the Derwent valley.

33. (below) Tunstall Reservoir in Weardale.

34. *(left) Cow Green Reservoir in Teesdale .*

35. *(above) Selset Reservoir in Lunedale, Teesdale.*

36. *(below) White-painted cottages in Upper Teesdale.*

Moving eastwards off the dales, the moorland gives way to lower hills and valleys. In the south, the River Tees flows through the gentle slopes of a wide plain. This is a pleasant rural area, full of attractive farms, villages and gardens. Over the fields and hedges, there are long, open views towards the hills of North Yorkshire.

This central, rolling plain extends northwards through the County. Glacial in origin, it has been the traditional artery of communication - the heart of the Land of the Prince Bishops. Whether by road, rail or on the waters of the River Wear itself, a rich tradition of trade and commerce is evident among the undulating fields and parklands. There are castles here and country houses. Against the green and well-kept countryside, their history is impressively displayed.

37. (right) Rolling landscape near Ferryhill.

38. (below) Harvest time in central County Durham.

39. *(above top) A typical County Durham haymeadow.*

40. *(above) Rokeby Park was built by Sir Thomas Robinson between 1725 and 1730.*

41. *(top right) Farmland near Sherburn.*

42. *(bottom right) Deep ponds near Darlington, glacial in origin and known as the 'Hell Kettles'.*

43. *(below) Many plants and animals have colonised the mineral-rich hills around Cassop Vale which is now a Site of Special Scientific Interest – as well as a beautiful and secluded place.*

The character of County Durham's heartland has also been strongly influenced by centuries of mining. It is a tribute to the skills and care of the population that much of the original beauty of the countryside has now been regained. The worst traces of the Industrial Revolution have been expunged and the former mining and ironworking communities bring an unusual, but unquestionably attractive, dimension to the landscape. The often isolated terraces of cottages have settled unfussily into the hillsides. The neat towns have followed the County-wide preference for green, open spaces and clear demarcation between settlements and countryside. The communities perch even on the highest places. Their presence is friendly and welcoming, one more contrast in this County of surprises.

44. *(far left) The dramatic setting of Lambton Castle evokes a rich history.*

45. *(left) A terrace of cottages in Weardale.*

46. *(below) A farm cottage in Weardale.*

47. (above) Cottages on one of Romaldkirk's village greens .

48. (left) Neat rows of Victorian terraced houses.

49. (below) Clear distinction between settlement and countryside, seen here at Sedgefield Village.

Between the Wear lowlands and the sea stands a north-south limestone escarpment. Unlike those in the west of the County, the limestones here are magnesian, yellow in colour rather than grey. They can be seen in quarries standing upon thick beds of sand - and, most noticeably, in the fabric of some older houses in the area.

This part of the County is characterised by low wooded ridges, established farmland and some delightful cottages and villages. Along the escarpment itself are patches of grassland and woodland in which survive rare plants. However it is behind the escarpment, where the land dips gently down to the buff-coloured cliffs of the coast, that greater secrets can be found.

The many streams tracing through the cliffs to the sea have cut narrow steep sided valleys known locally as 'denes'. The private, wooded world of the denes contrasts strongly with the open slopes above - and sometimes with each other. One may offer enough adventure and surprises for any child. Another a shady haven for walking. A third a naturalist's paradise, a home for rare plants and many species of birds. It is here, in the Castle Eden Dene, that the rare Durham Argus butterfly can be found.

50. (top) The limestone escarpment near Sherburn.

51. (above left) Bird life at the mouth of Castle Eden Dene.

52. (left) The coast at Seaham.

53. *(left) A field of poppies near Plawsworth.*

54. *(above) Foxholes Dene.*

55. *(right) Hawthorn Dene.*

56. *(below Left) Himalayan Balsam.*

57. *(below right) Bird's-foot Trefoil and Bloody Cranesbill.*

58. *(bottom left) Bladderwort.*

59. *(bottom right) Great Bellflower.*

Perhaps the most intriguing feature of the denes is the way in which they appear to have responded to man's occupation of the coast. A number of the villages along the coast derive from the days of mining - and yet the denes appear to have sliced around and under the communities as if the collieries had stood there for many more centuries than they actually have. Castle Eden Dene, for example, penetrates to the heart of the town of Peterlee, but not yet through it.

In fact only two of more than one hundred collieries now remain. Different industries are beginning to find their niche in the coastal infrastructure - blending with the environment, not confronting it. Throughout the area, however, the tradition of close-knit communities and unambiguous boundaries endures. The traveller can chart his progress without hesitation from one community to the next, though little more than a field may separate them. The street names evoke images of a powerful industrial history. This windswept coast breeds strength and resilience - and yet respect for tradition, too.

The values of the Prince Bishops are discernible today upon the face of the landscape of County Durham. Resourcefulness and good husbandry have turned the remaining legacies of industrial history into places of continuing fascination, and have harmonised them with the environment. Careful planting has done much to restore the deciduous woodlands and early character of the land. The scenery both surprises and stimulates.

This is indeed superb country.

60. (far left) Castle Eden Dene.

61. (above left) Wingate Quarry – once a major contributor of building stone and lime but now a nature reserve.

62. (left) The 'castle' at Castle Eden.

Early History

63. (left) Binchester Roman Fort.

64. (above) Remains of the Roman Fort at Lanchester.

People have dwelt in the hills and valleys between the Rivers Tyne and Tees for thousands of years - long before the area became known as County Durham. Of those who lived here before the Romans came, we know little. The tools of Stone Age fishermen are occasionally found along the coast. Stone arrowheads and axeheads tell us, too, that people were travelling regularly through Weardale around 2000 BC. Later immigrants from the low countries - known as the 'Beaker' people from the shape of their short-necked pots - left examples of their work in the area of the villages of Brandon and Sacriston.

Tools and weapons of bronze have also been found in Heathery Burn Cave near Stanhope. These have been dated at around 700 BC and are now displayed in the British Museum, evidence that some of Britain's earliest metal workers lived in the Durham Dales. Few traces remain, however, of those who later brought the techniques of ironworking into Britain. This is probably because the people of the north were semi-nomadic.

The Romans

By the time of the arrival of the Romans in 43 AD, the lands around Durham formed part of the territory of the Brigantes. The Romans settled first in southern Britain and for some years ignored the north. Relations between the Brigantes and their Roman neighbours blew hot and cold until the Roman governor, Agricola, finally conquered the northern tribes in about 80 AD.

A Roman road, later known as Dere Street, was built northwards from York to the Firth of Forth in Scotland. Forts were erected at each of the main river crossings in the Durham region - at Piercebridge (Magis) on the Tees, at Binchester (Vinovia) on the Wear, and at Ebchester (Vindomora) on the Derwent. A fort was also built at Lanchester (Longovicium). Of note, too, is the inclusion of Binchester and the River Wear (Vedra) in Ptolemy's geography of the known world, published in the 2nd Century AD.

More forts were built at Greta Bridge (Maglona) and Bowes (Lavatrae) where the Roman route from Scotch Corner to the west passed through County Durham. Signal stations followed the route towards Stainmore. There was also a small fortlet at Rey Cross, close to the County boundary with Cumbria. To the east of Dere Street, the route from the Humber to the bridge over the Tyne at Newcastle passed through Chester le Street (Concangium) before branching north-eastwards to the Roman port at South Shields.

65. (above) Part of the Roman Fort at Piercebridge – the village is built almost entirely within the limits of the fort.

Small civilian communities gathered around the forts. Numerous traces of their life and industry testify that Roman civilisation became well established in the area. The remains of aqueducts, bath houses and central heating systems have been found and also lime kilns and one of the most northerly villa estates known in the Roman world (Old Durham, near Durham City). The impressive Roman collection at The Bowes Museum, Barnard Castle, contains many examples of Roman ornaments and coins.

Yet Durham remained only a frontier district of the Roman Empire, just south of the Emperor Hadrian's famous wall. By 410 AD, the Roman legions had withdrawn. The way was now open for the next wave of invaders.

66. (top) Hypocaust at Binchester — the under-floor heating system by which the three rooms of the bath house were heated to progressively higher temperatures.

67. (above) A large, ancient encampment on the edge of Hamsterley Forest, known locally as 'The Castles'.

68. *(above) An ancient route-marker at Muggleswick.*

69. *(below) The Church of St John The Evangelist at Escomb dates from the 7th Century and was built with stone removed from the Roman Fort at Binchester.*

The Anglo-Saxons

Angles and Saxons from Denmark and northern Germany settled along the Northumberland Coast and in the Tyne valley during the 5th and 6th Centuries. In his writings about that period, Simeon of Durham tells us that the land between the Tyne and the Tees was 'a deserted waste . . . nothing but a hiding place for wild and woodland beasts'. By the end of the 6th Century, however, it had become firmly part of Aethelfrith's kingdom of Northumbria: the northern half of his realm, Bernicia, probably covered present day Northumberland and County Durham; the southern half, Deira, most of Yorkshire.

During the 7th and 8th Centuries, the Angles or 'English' began to tame Simeon's 'deserted waste'. They established villages in places like Wolsingham, Cleatlam, Easington, Darlington and Hunwick. In time, the pagan invaders were themselves tamed by Christian missionaries. Paulinus of York baptised King Edwin of Northumbria in 627. A little later, King Oswald invited Aidan to leave the Celtic Christian settlement on Iona and establish a monastic community on the island of Lindisfarne, off the Northumberland coast. One of his successors as Bishop of Lindisfarne was the Anglian Cuthbert. Indeed, the conflict between Roman and Celtic traditions ended at the synod of Whitby in 664 and, in its wake, art and literature blossomed in the north east of England.

Benedictine monasteries were founded at Monkwearmouth and Jarrow by Benedict Biscop at the end of the 7th Century.

70. (above left) Sundial on the wall of Escomb's Anglo-Saxon church.

71. (left) Escomb Church's sundial in close-up.

From the age of seven, the Venerable Bede (674-735), 'the father of English history', lived in these two monasteries, producing his 'Ecclesiastical History of the English Church and People'. Miraculously, the church of St John the Evangelist at Escomb has survived from those times, built with Roman masonry from the nearby fort of Vinovia. In Durham Castle, there are also examples of the sculpture of the period.

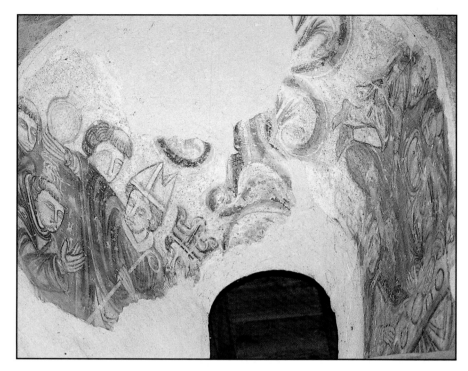

72. *(right) Wall paintings of St Cuthbert at St Lawrence's, Pittington.*

73. *(below) The tomb of The Venerable Bede in Durham Cathedral.*

The Vikings

In 793, this peaceful world was shattered by Viking raids from Denmark. Buildings were looted and burned although the Northumbrian churches were left intact for a further 70 years. In 866, however, the monasteries of Jarrow and Wearmouth were destroyed, and in 875, the Lindisfarne community left its island home to wander for seven years carrying the body of St Cuthbert. Eventually, in 882, the community settled at Chester le Street and built its church on the site of the present parish church. The Scandinavian rulers of Yorkshire ratified the rights of St Cuthbert's followers over the lands between the Tyne and the Tees - and the origins of the County of Durham were thereby established.

However, the trials and tribulations of the Community of St Cuthbert were not yet over. The monks were later driven out of Chester le Street and forced south as far as Ripon in Yorkshire. We are told that, during the journey back, the Saint's coffin became fixed to the ground and that, in a vision, the travellers were bidden to transport it to Dunholm, the 'hill island'. They followed a girl who was looking for her dun cow - an incident commemorated in a carving on the Cathedral wall - and found the naturally defended peninsula of Durham.

Here, in 999, a shrine was finally erected for St Cuthbert's body. The Earl of Northumbria, Uchtred, brought in artisans to help build the stone edifice which became known as the White Church. The bones of Bede were later brought from Jarrow and the shrine itself became an important place of pilgrimage. Among its early visitors was King Canute.

74. (above left) The Church of St Mary and St Cuthbert, Chester le Street.

75. *(left) The 'peninsula', Durham City.*

76. *(right) Today's Dun Cow Lane in Durham City connects the Bailey with Palace Green.*

77. *(below) Rey Cross on the western boundary of County Durham with Cumbria marks the spot where Eric Bloodaxe, the last great Viking King of York, was killed by Earl Maccus at the Battle of Stainmore.*

78. *(below right) Durham City walls, St Cuthbert's Walk.*

The Normans

Following the Norman invasion of 1066, the northern English rebelled against William the Conqueror. He, in turn, retaliated with the devastation and massacre known as 'the harrying of the north'. William also sought to exploit the religious power and prestige of the See of St Cuthbert in order to secure a greater measure of control over the local population and also as a defensive measure against the Scots. In 1071, therefore, he appointed Walcher as Bishop of Durham. Walcher's career advanced further in 1075 when he became Earl of Northumberland, with jurisdiction between the Tees and the Scottish border.

William and his successor, William Rufus, gave more land in the region to other faithful Norman retainers. The Count of Brittany was made Earl of Richmond for his efforts at the Battle of Hastings; he marked his territory by building a castle at Bowes on the site of the Roman fort (the castle was later replaced by one built for Henry II). Guy de Baliol was endowed with land in Teesdale where fortifications built by his son gave the name to the town of Barnard Castle.

79. *(left) The castle at Barnard Castle.*

80. *(above) Bowes Castle.*

81. *(below) The 13th Century Church of St Helen's at Kelloe.*

The power of the Bishops of Durham was considerable. They maintained their own armies, minted their own coins, owned all the mines and resembled more closely the Prince Bishops of Germany than senior English clerics. That the Domesday Survey stopped short of the County boundary and did not encroach upon the See is perhaps a reflection of just how influential the Bishops of Durham were becoming.

Bishops of such stature and importance needed a castle to live in - and Bishop Walcher started to build his upon the steep rock in Durham around which loops the River Wear. It was an easy site to defend and the structure withstood Danish attacks in 1075. The most impressive and best preserved of Norman castles in the whole country, it is now owned by the University of Durham. The Castle, including the Norman Chapel and Gallery and the 13th Century Great Hall are open to the public for guided tours.

Bishop Walcher's successor was William de St Calais. He made a lasting impact with his favoured

82. *(top left) The Cloisters and West Towers.*

84. *(above) Durham Castle and Cathedral.*

83. *(bottom left) Durham Cathedral from Leazes Road.*

85. *(below) Prebends' Bridge was built in 1772-5 at the expense of the Canons or Prebends of Durham Cathedral – it replaced a narrow footbridge which had been destroyed in the Great Flood of 1771.*

86. (left) Durham Cathedral from the river bank.

87. (above) The Courtyard of Durham Castle.

building project, which was the magnificent Cathedral of Durham itself. Having seen many new churches in Normandy during temporary exile there, Bishop William dismantled Durham's Saxon church in 1092 and started to build afresh in 1093. Most of the construction was completed within 40 years.

According to Nikolaus Pevsner, 'Durham is one of the great experiences of Europe . . . The group of cathedral, castle and monastery on the rock can only be compared to Avignon and Prague.' Today, the excellence of the site has been justly recognised by the award of World Heritage Site status. The atmosphere and history of the place have been best articulated by Sir Walter Scott. These words are engraved upon Prebends' Bridge, below the Cathedral itself:

Grey towers of Durham
Yet well I love thy mixed
and massive piles
Half church of God, half
castle 'gainst the Scot
And long to roam these
venerable aisles
With records stored of deeds
long since forgot

The Middle Ages

88. (left) Legs Cross is on the western side of the old
Roman road of Dere Street – its purpose is uncertain but
it may well have been a route marker for the increasing
trade in the County.

89. (above) The remains of the pele tower at Ludworth
(early 15th Century).

The Prince Bishops continued to flourish during the Middle Ages. Bishop Hugh de Puiset (whose name has been anglicised to 'Pudsey') amassed great wealth. Some of his possessions, including his beautifully illuminated Bible, are among the silver plate and other church furnishings on display in the Cathedral Treasury. In 1189, he purchased the Earldom, Manor and Wapentake of Sadberge, a tract of land on the north bank of the Tees. The purchase price was £11,000 which brought the right to add an earl's coronet to the arms of the Bishopric.

In order to supervise his lands effectively, de Puiset carried out his own 'Domesday' survey of the County in 1180. The results are contained in The Boldon Book. The survey tells us something of the developments in agriculture and the reorganisation of estates since the earlier devastation. Many of the County's distinctive open village greens and commons date from this period. The farming was mostly pastoral although corn was grown around Darlington and there were forests in the west - a familiar picture. Most of the population was under some obligation to the Bishops - fencing, carrying, helping with hunts, even mining. Mineral exploitation occurred in the west where de Puiset had royal permission to mine silver and lead in Weardale. Iron ore was also extracted. Although coal was already being worked, the ore was smelted and forged with charcoal.

We do not know the details of those who worked the enterprises although the names and exploits of the lords of the manors are well recorded. Members of two local families actually became kings of Scotland, Robert de Brus of Hartlepool and John de Baliol of Barnard Castle.

Others influenced English history, particularly the Nevilles of Raby and Brancepeth. Ralph Neville, whose tomb is in Staindrop Church, beat the Scots at Nevilles Cross in 1346. The family later became Earls of Westmorland and were deeply involved in Plantagenet politics during the Wars of the Roses. Indeed, it was Cecily, a daughter of the house and famous as 'The Rose of Raby', who married the Duke of York. Two of her sons became Edward IV and Richard III.

90. *(above) Deer in the grounds of Raby Castle.*

91. *(below) Raby Castle in Teesdale.*

The Nevilles eventually fell from power having chosen to support Mary, Queen of Scots, in the Rising of the North against Elizabeth I in 1569. The Baron's Hall, where this ill-fated plot was hatched, was later described by Wordsworth:

Seven hundred knights, retainers all of Neville, at their master's call had sate together at Raby's Hall.

Raby Castle, set in beautiful parkland, is now open to the public. The Baron's Hall and sumptuous state rooms contain fine period furniture and paintings while, outside, a collection of horse-drawn carriages is housed in the Palladian stables. The Nevilles' other castle at Brancepeth is still standing, too. However, much of what can be seen at Brancepeth today, including the 'chessmen' gate towers, is a 19th Century imitation commissioned by a wealthy family of coal owners, the Russells.

92. *(above) Brancepeth Castle.*

93. *(right) Witton Castle, Weardale.*

94. (above) Lumley Castle, Chester le Street.

95. (left) 18th Century Stanhope Castle now converted into private accommodation occupies the site of a fortress built by Bishop Beck at the beginning of the 14th Century.

96. (below) Elvet Bridge over the River Wear at Durham City was originally built in the 12th Century, chapels stood at either end of the bridge.

Other great families were the Lumleys, the Hyltons and the Eures. In the 14th and 15th Centuries, licences were issued to fortify their castles at Lumley, Hylton and Witton le Wear. Lumley is still an impressive, square-towered, late 14th Century building with a few later alterations by Sir John Vanbrugh. The castle is at present used as an hotel but remains in the ownership of the Lumley family, now Earls of Scarbrough.

Witton Castle, formerly home of the Eures, is now owned by the Lambtons. Lambton Castle itself, however, which stands on the site of Harraton Hall, is another 19th Century romantic creation. The family came from Lambton Old Hall on the opposite bank of the River Wear. This was the home of John Lambton who, legend has it, killed the 'Lambton Worm', an evil serpent which terrorised the neighbourhood. A descendant was John George Lambton, first Earl of Durham and the High Commissioner and Governor General of Canada in 1838-9. It was in his memory that a

monument was erected at nearby Penshaw; the 'Greek Doric' temple can be seen from all over the north of the County.

Less well-known families built their houses on a more modest scale: Stanhope Hall; Crook Hall in Durham City; Witton Tower, originally a defended pele tower. Also of interest is the restored and privately owned East Deanery, once the home of the Dean of St Andrew, Bishop Auckland.

Successive bishops, too, left their mark upon the County in the form of fine churches, bridges and hospitals. Bishop Flambard founded Kepier Hospital and built Durham's city walls and the Framwellgate Bridge. Bishop de Puiset founded Sherburn Hospital and constructed Elvet Bridge and St Cuthbert's Church in Darlington - one of the most important Early English churches in the north of England. He also started to build a new palace at Bishop Auckland. Set in parkland and complete with a Gothic cloister to shelter the deer, Auckland Castle is now the permanent residence of the Bishops of Durham.

97. (above) 98. (below) The Bishop's Palace at Bishop Auckland.

The County's two ruined monastic buildings also date from this period. The hermit and former seafarer, St Godric, settled at Finchale in 1110. This was later the site of Finchale Priory which was built in the early 13th Century. A similarly peaceful riverside setting was chosen for the abbey at Egglestone, which was painted by Turner and eulogised by Scott.

Ecclesiastical influence can be seen in other place names up and down the County - Bishop Middleham, Bishopton, Sacriston. A Norman flavour is also detectable. Bearpark, for example, derives from beau repaire, the beautiful retreat of the Prior of Durham. Beamish (Bewmys) and Butterby (Beutroue) have been similarly anglicised. Once prominent local lords are also remembered in the names Witton Gilbert, Hutton Henry and Coatham Mundeville.

99. (above) 100. (below) Finchale Priory once served as a retreat for monks from Durham Cathedral – small groups would be sent out periodically to join the resident friars.

101. (above) Egglestone Abbey was founded in 1190 by the White Canons of the Premonstratensian Order – they took their names from their distinctive white clothing.

103. (right) Kepier Farm near Durham City where a hospital was founded in 1112 by Bishop de Puiset – it was attacked by the Scots in 1306 and by the plague in 1351.

102. (below) The Pack Horse Bridge, Hag Bridge at Eggleston.

Slowly the towns began to grow.
Licences to hold markets were
granted in Durham City,
Darlington, Sedgefield, Staindrop,
Wolsingham and in Barnard Castle
where a fine early town house,
Blagraves, still survives. Durham
City, which received its charter in
1180, Darlington and Bishop
Auckland, gradually emerged as
the major centres. However, they
still remained small towns - partly,
perhaps, because the Bishops
feared any municipal challenge to
their authority.

Their growth may also have been
checked by constant border
warfare. Having been earlier
sacked by William the Conqueror,
who 'left not a house standing
between York and Durham', the
County was laid waste once more
by David I of Scotland who put his
own nominee in the Bishop's
palace in 1140. Again in 1217, the
Scots invaded. In 1297, however,
the spirit of St Cuthbert is reputed
to have helped stop a fresh
invasion at the Tyne. At the start of
the 14th Century, a new threat
from the north was bought off but
attacks continued in almost every
decade until the Battle of Nevilles

104. (left) *The Sanctuary Knocker on the door of Durham Cathedral.*

105. (bottom left) *The haunted ruins of Langley Hall, near Witton Gilbert, dating from the early 16th Century.*

106. (below) *The remains of Dalden Tower in Dalton le Dale – a fortification dating from the time of Edward II.*

Cross in 1346. Then, forty years later, the Scots came south once more to plunder.

A ruinous combination of repeated pillage, of crop failures, famine and plague, led unsurprisingly to economic and population decline. Villages disappeared and lawlessness prevailed. Although many criminals were caught and dealt with at the Palatinate's own court, others claimed sanctuary by clasping the great knocker of the Cathedral door. The days of singular privilege were ending.

In 1536, Henry VIII finally deprived the Bishops of Durham of their right to administer civil and criminal law, to collect taxes and to mint Palatinate coinage. In the same year, a rebellion against the break with Rome and against the removal of Palatinate powers - known as 'the Pilgrimage of Grace' - was joined by all the major County families except the Eures. But the rebellion failed. The shrines of St Cuthbert and the Venerable Bede were despoiled in 1537 and the monastery dissolved in 1539.

The 17th to 19th Centuries

107. *(left) The signs of enclosure – dry-stone walls and large fields in Upper Teesdale . . .*

108. *(above) . . . and also in Weardale.*

The times became more settled. Prompted particularly by demand from an increasing population of miners, much was done to improve agriculture and increase food production. Walls and fences broke up the huge, open common fields. The face of the countryside had begun to change and the skills and inventiveness of the people quickly followed suit.

Between 1550 and 1750, town fields were progressively enclosed. Later it was the turn of the upland fells where evidence of the process - straight roads, large fields and dry-stone walls - can be very clearly seen today in the Lanchester area. In the communities themselves, the achievements were considerable. Years of breeding shorthorn cattle for the production of meat for the table and fat for soap and candle-making led in the 1790s to the Durham Ox - a splendid specimen raised by the Colling brothers at Ketton near Darlington. The ox weighed nearly a ton and a half and was exhibited throughout the country. Sheep breeds were also improved to provide more meat and wool. Craft industries prospered, for example linen-making on the Tees. A Durham company manufactured table mustard for the first time and made this new and exciting condiment nationally famous.

Prosperity grew and the richer families built themselves handsome country houses, many of which still adorn the County. The foundations of Gainford Hall were laid in 1600 by the Reverend John Cradock. Horden Hall, of the same period, was built by the Conyers family while the Edens of West Auckland Hall raised yet another illustrious County Durham line: George Eden, first Earl of Auckland, became Governor- General of New Zealand and gave the name to Auckland in North Island; and Sir Anthony Eden, of course, became Prime Minister.

Of note, too, are Westernhopeburn in Weardale, Westholme near Winston, Unthank Hall at Stanhope and Whitfield Place in Wolsingham - all fine 17th Century houses. A century later, the similarly impressive Bishop Oak Hall and Whitfield House had been added to the district of Wolsingham.

109. (above) Whitfield House, Wolsingham .

110. (below) Wolsingham in Weardale.

111. *(above) Horsley Hall in Weardale.*

112. *(below) Westernhopeburn Farm in Weardale.*

The mining industry was also growing throughout the period. Silver and lead had actually been worked in the west since certainly the Middle Ages if not earlier. Coal had also been mined during the 13th and 14th centuries and transported by sea to distant markets. In 1583, the diocese granted a 99 year lease of the manors of Gateshead and Whickham to Elizabeth I who, in turn, assigned it to two Newcastle entrepreneurs. Many coal mines had already come under the control of Newcastle entrepreneurs and the acquisition of the great mines of Gateshead and Whickham assured Newcastle's dominance over the coal trade. The so-called 'Grand Lease' afforded them the right to regulate the coal trade.

In addition to jobs for the miners, the industry brought fortune and honour for the coal owners. Rivalries grew between them to the extent that, during the Civil War, Newcastle was Royalist while Sunderland identified with Parliament. The industry itself, however continued to advance and spread. Transporting the coal, first to the river estuaries and then by sea to southern markets, stimulated both ship and wagonway building. By the end of the 17th Century, coalmining was at the core of a highly integrated, industrial system.

The advent of the new breed of entrepreneurs was marked by political change. The County had already tasted social change as some of the older families, like the Nevilles, were supplanted by new names such as the Vanes. However, traditions had still not changed enough for the likes of certain of the new merchant families. The Lilburnes, for example, were distinctly radical in their outlook. Robert Lilburne, Squire of Thickley, was a contemporary and supporter of Cromwell - and, for a time, his Commander in Chief in Scotland. He was also a signatory of Charles I's death warrant. His brother, John Lilburne, was leader of the 'Levellers', a group of people with an intense belief in religious and social equality.

The restoration of the monarchy saw a return of a strong episcopal influence in the County, with Bishops like Cosin and Crewe. The former was famous for his charitable work, including the repair of the chapel at Auckland Castle and encouragement of improvement in parish churches. It was only after Cosin's death, that Durham was allowed to send Members of Parliament to the House of Commons. In 1673, two were sent from the County and two from the City. Previously, parliamentary representation had only been achieved during Cromwell's protectorate or by way of the Bishop's seat in the House of Lords. Among the County's early MPs was 'Bonny Bobby Shafto' of Whitworth Hall, whose election song is known now as a nursery rhyme.

Nathaniel, Lord Crewe, succeeded Cosin as Bishop. He was an ardent supporter of James II and tried to introduce into the County the King's policy of support for non - conformists. However, he found himself isolated and, in 1688, he switched allegiance from James to his opponent and successor, William of Orange. The church's influence gradually declined - and the names of Vane, Tempest and Lambton began to figure more prominently in the chronicles of the County.

113. *(Above left) A colliery recreated at the North of England Open Air Museum, Beamish.*

114. *(left) High on the western slopes of the Hudeshope Valley north of Middleton in Teesdale, the Coldberry Lead Mine was to produce nearly 2000 tons of ore for local smelt mills.*

115. *(below) Vane Tempest Hall, Gilesgate. The last surviving example of a militia barracks in County Durham.*

The new squirearchy built themselves elegant houses. Freville Lambton constructed the dignified Biddick Hall, influenced possibly by Sir John Vanbrugh. In 1749-53, Elemore Hall near Pittington was built in a mixture of Palladian and Baroque styles. Both Elemore Hall and Croxdale Hall contain fine plasterwork thought to be the work of the Italian craftsman, Guiseppe Cortese. St Helen Hall and Auckland Castle also have notable plaster ceilings.

Many pleasant Georgian country houses have survived from the 18th Century including those at Hurworth, Beamish and Castle Eden. Hamsterley Hall is a charming example of Georgian 'gothick' (mounted on the Hall's front lawn, incidentally, is a pinnacle taken from the Victorian

116. (right) The Market Cross or Buttermarket, Barnard Castle.

117. (below) The Bowes Museum, Barnard Castle.

118. (far right) Cottages in Cotherstone, Teesdale.

Palace of Westminster during its restoration in the 1930s). The classical style of architecture continued to be popular in the early 19th Century. Its most distinguished practitioner in the County was Ignatius Bonomi who designed Burn Hall and Eggleston Hall. Rokeby Park is also of note.

With the increase in prosperity, better housing became more wide-spread and fashionable. Using local skills and local materials, many simple but attractive houses were built around the village greens. Barningham is one good example. In picturesque Romaldkirk, the houses cluster around the 12th Century 'kirk' of St Romuald in a pattern of delightful, interconnecting greens. Particularly noteworthy was the practice of building cottages as well as houses - even today a good and harmonious cross-section of accommodation is generally apparent in County Durham's rural communities.

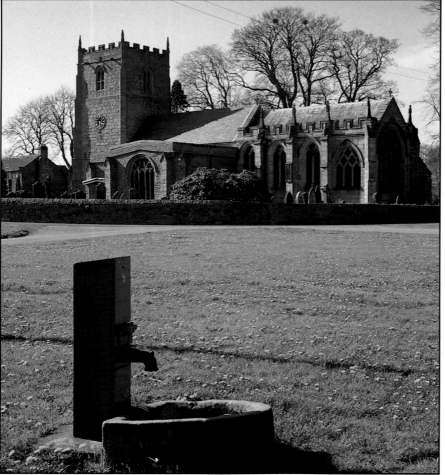

119. (above) Romaldkirk – the old village stocks can be seen on one of the village greens . . .

120. (left) . . . while nearby is the village pump.

121. (right) Eggleston Hall in Teesdale.

More fine 18th and 19th Century homes can be found in Gainford and Hurworth, both in lower Teesdale, while Durham City and Barnard Castle have the best collections of town houses from the period. Durham City has many handsome Georgian examples, while the lovely market town of Barnard Castle has quite a variety in its wide streets: a dramatic ruined castle and a fascinating collection of historic buildings dating from the 16th Century. These include weavers' cottages with their attic workshop windows; the Market Cross of 1747; and The Bowes Museum built in the 1870s and 1880s in the style of a French chateau.

The period has indeed bequeathed a rich legacy of architecture to the County. To the significant developments in housing should be added many important public and ecclesiastical buildings. Ushaw College near Durham City, for example, which was built between 1804 and 1819, and progressively extended from 1837. Bishop Auckland's town hall is also notable. Built in 1860-2, the building has a curious French character and stands in the middle of the market place. The weekly market still takes place, overlooked by town houses of the 18th and 19th Centuries.

122. (above right) The Deer House at Auckland Park – built by Bishop Trevor in 1760.

123. (right) Auckland Park.

124. (far right) Gardens are an important part of Durham's villages.

125. (above) A typically attractive village garden.

126. (above right) Owengate is the main street between Durham Castle and Cathedral and the Bailey – it has strong ecclesiastical and legal links.

127. (far right) Bow Lane in Durham City was once called Kingsgate – William the Conqueror is alleged to have fled from the City along this street, unnerved at the prospect of viewing St Cuthbert's Relics.

128. (right) Pimlico in Durham City.

129. (above) South Bailey, Durham City, is believed by many enthusiasts of Georgian architecture to be one of the most attractive streets in the country – it has a wide variety of door fronts and fanlights.

130. (right) The Ramp in Durham City was reputedly an ancient entry from the river bank into the monastery – in order to combat intruders, the 'Dark Entry' as it was so called was designed in such a way as to leave exposed the unprotected right side of the body (it was assumed that the shield would always be on the left).

131. (above right) South Street once formed part of the main north-south road through Durham City – this ancient street retains its cobbled surface.

132. (far right) The view towards Elvet Bridge from Durham City.

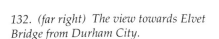

133. (left) The House of Correction, Elvet Bridge, was in use from 1632 to 1819.

135. (below) Seaham Hall was once the home of the wealthy Milbanke family – there Lord Byron married Anne Isabella Milbanke on 2 January 1815. Later Seaham Hall and its estate was purchased by the Marquess of Londonderry.

134. (above) Shotton Hall in Peterlee is a fine example of a late 18th Century country house – it is said to be haunted by the ghost of a grief-stricken servant girl who suffered at the hands of an early owner.

The Industrial Revolution

136. *(left) The old drinking fountain in Middleton in Teesdale.*

137. *(above) The small shop fronts remain in Middleton in Teesdale.*

138. *(below) The Stanhope and Weardale Cooperative Society in Frosterley.*

Once the part-time occupation of many a dale farmer, lead-mining assumed increasing importance on the slopes of Teesdale and Weardale during the 18th Century. The physical extent of the developing industry can be glimpsed today from the hillside scars of a process known as 'hushing'. New veins of ore were exposed by releasing dammed watercourses which washed away the topsoil. The Quaker London Lead Company established a northern head-quarters in thriving Middleton in Teesdale, providing houses, schools and medical facilities in return for sober diligence. However the hazards were great and the existence punishing. To those risks normally associated with mining could be added pneumonia and rheumatism from the harsh climate.

By the middle of the 19th Century, lead-dressing - the separation of ore from waste - had been mechanised. New machinery was installed by the Blackett Beaumont Company at their Park Level Mine at Killhope in Weardale. The mill was powered by a great iron water wheel, 34 feet (10 metres) in diameter, which can still be seen turning again today by vistors to The Killhope Lead Mining Centre.

139. (right) Killhope Wheel.

140. (below) Killhope Lead Mining Centre.

141. (top far right) Killhope Wheel.

142. (bottom far right) The miners' appalling living conditions as portrayed at Killhope.

143. (Top left) 144. (bottom left)
145. (left) Remains of the Slit Mine at Slit Wood in Weardale – the valley was so narrow that the burn had to be covered to provide extra space for machinery.

146. (below) The scars of lead 'hushing' remain in the form of artificially created valleys – these were caused by damming up a burn and then releasing the flow of water which washed away the topsoil and exposed the veins of lead.

The County was always best known for its coal. At first, it was worked in the shallowest seams in the west, often by 'drifts' from the surface wherever the coal outcropped. Shafts were later sunk to reach the deeper seams. By 1650, depths of 400 feet (120 metres) were not uncommon but, in order to go deeper, new techniques of draining and ventilation were becoming necessary. In the early 18th Century, therefore, the Newcomen steam engine was introduced to pump out the mines. This was an important milestone in the industry.

Once on the surface, the coal had to be transported. At first, it was carried in horse-drawn 'chaldron' wagons and, later, in wagons pulled by huge cables worked by stationary steam engines. The County's landscape was criss-crossed by these wagonways, one of which was carried across the Causey Burn by the world's oldest surviving railway bridge, built in 1725-26. A traveller from the south, a Mr Howitt, was fascinated by them:

Here and there, you saw careering over the plain, long trains of coal waggons, without horses or attendants or any apparent cause of motion but their own mad agency. They seemed, indeed, rather driven or dragged by unseen demons.

Mr Howitt's 'unseen demons' were no more than long wire ropes. They were progressively replaced by steam railway locomotives which, from their birthplace in the north east of England, were to take power and industry all over the world.

147. (top right) Dales Ponies in Teesdale – these good-looking natives of the North East Pennine dales were originally used as pack ponies for the lead mining industry.

148. (above right) A 'chaldron' wagon now preserved at Causey Arch.

149. (right) Lime Kiln at Ireshope Moor, Weardale, used for making agricultural and industrial lime – limestone was packed into the kiln while the base was filled with layers of coal and wood, and then ignited.

Three local men dominated early railway history. George Stephenson developed the steam locomotive. Timothy Hackworth, a skilled engineer, built and modified engines at his Soho works in Shildon. Edward Pease provided the initiative and cash for the historic Stockton and Darlington Railway, the first passenger railway in the world.

The new railway opened on 27 September 1825. The engine - called 'Locomotion' - drew 80 tons of coal, engineers and committee men at between 10 and 12 miles per hour. 'Locomotion' is now on display at the Darlington Railway Centre and Museum while a replica occassionally puffs along the tracks at the North of England Open Air Museum at Beamish. Two of Hackworth's engines can be viewed at the Hackworth Museum in Shildon. They include a replica of 'Sans Pareil', which was beaten by Stephenson's 'Rocket' in the Rainhill Locomotive Trials in 1829.

150. (above) 'Locomotion'.

151. (below) Opened in 1857, this Victorian viaduct is one of Durham City's prominent landmarks.

152. (below) *The opening of the Stockton and Darlington Railway, 1825*
Watercolour by John Dobbin (1815 – 1888).

GENERAL
TOM THUMB
The American Man in Miniature.

Under the Patronage of Her Majesty, H. R. H. Prince Albert, the Queen Dowager, H. R. H. the Duchess of Kent, the King and Queen of the Belgians, the Dukes of

...re, Buckingham, the Nobility generally, and visited in London ...RSONS, in the space of Four Months.

Cambridge, We..."

This extraordinary little Gentleman was born in the United States of America, and is accompanied hither by his Parents, Guardian, and Preceptor. He is in his Thirteenth year, IS SMALLER THAN ANY INFANT THAT EVER WALKED ALONE, and

WEIGHS ONLY FIFTEEN POUNDS!

The GENERAL will have the honour of holding his Public Levees

AT THE ASSEMBLY ROOM, SUN INN, DARLINGTON,
On Monday, November 4th. 1844,
DAY AND EVENING,

Positively for ONE DAY only, as he exhibits in DURHAM on the 5th.

GENERAL TOM THUMB will relate his History, sing a variety of SONGS, appear in various DANCES, &c. He will also give an Imitation of

Napoleon in full Military Costume,
AND
THE GRECIAN STATUES!

The little GENERAL will likewise appear in the magnificent COURT DRESS which he had the honour of wearing THREE TIMES before HER MAJESTY at BUCKINGHAM PALACE, and also before the QUEEN DOWAGER at Marlborough House.

The MAGNIFICENT PRESENTS given him by HER MAJESTY, the QUEEN DOWAGER, the DUKE of DEVONSHIRE, &c., will be exhibited. The GENERAL will also dispose of his MEMOIRS (6d. each,) and his LIKENESS, with fac-similes of his Autograph, giving STAMPED RECEIPTS, to LADIES only.

The GENERAL's New & Elegant CARRIAGE, drawn by two of the Smallest Ponies in the World, with Coachman and Footman, in Splendid Liveries, will pass through the Streets, Weather permitting.

Hours of Exhibition, from 11 *to* 1 ; 3 *to* 5 ; *and* 7 *to* 9.

Doors open Half-an-Hour previous.

Admission, One Shilling, regardless of age.

Printed by W. Oliver, Market-place, Darlington.

Darlington grew and prospered with the achievements of entrepreneurs such as the Peases and the Backhouses. These two important Quaker families built or bequeathed many fine buildings including the well-known clock tower which stands high above the Market Hall. The Friends' Meeting House in Skinnergate is further evidence of Quaker influence within the town: like Pease's own house it has been recently restored.

Building the first railways led to further pioneering developments in the County. The first iron railway bridge ever to be constructed has been reassembled in the National Railway Museum, York. Also built to cross the River Gaunless near West Auckland was the first 'skewed' railway bridge. Next came many magnificent viaducts, such as that at Hownes Gill, two miles south of Consett.

In truth, an exhilarating reversal of centuries of experience was happening. Having been cut-off from the rest of the country - deliberately so under some of the Bishops - County Durham now found itself at the leading edge of the Industrial Revolution. By the middle of the 19th Century, the pace of invention and industrialisation was increasing and the whole of the north east was in a ferment of expectation. The first friction match was invented at Stockton and the first coke by-product plant established at Crook in County Durham. Further developments included iron ships, screw propulsion, the first tanker, turbines and the incandescent lamp.

153. (far left) 'Sans Pareil'.

154. (left) A sample of evening entertainment in 19th Century Darlington.

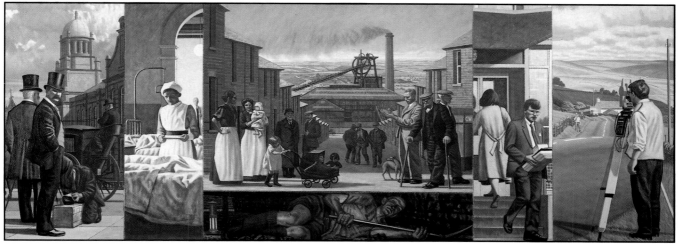

155. (left) This striking mural in South Hetton
commemorates the community's 152 years of total dependence
upon its colliery.

156. (above) The Durham County Council Centenary
Painting by Julian Cooper, 1989, conveys much local history
and atmosphere.

Many of these developments were a direct consequence of the growth of the coalmining industry. In order to move the coal from colliery to market place, railways were built and staithes and coal-drops constructed at the coal port. Seaham Harbour, for example, was built by Lord Londonderry specifically for the export of his own coal. Most of the collier ships were also built in the region thus creating a demand for iron plates.

By 1860, County Durham had 58 ironworks with blast furnaces. The largest were at Spennymoor, Darlington, Witton Park, Seaham, Tow Law and Consett. It was scarcely surprising, therefore, that in the second half of the 19th Century two out of every five ships in the world had been built in the north east of England. By the end of the Century, Spennymoor had the largest plate mill in Europe and the Consett Iron Works, which had been founded by the Derwent Iron Company in 1839, dominated the area. In fact, Consett's association with iron had started much earlier and the arrival of swordsmiths from Solingen in Germany during the late 17th Century had brought many skilled craftsmen to the area. The Derwentcote steel furnace was constructed near Rowland's Gill.

The railway engines, the ships and the ironworks themselves all needed fuel and the demand for coal continued to grow into the present Century. In 1911, with the introduction of new cutting machines to supplement traditional 'hand-hewing', production from the Durham coalfield reached a peak of over 41 million tons.

However, the rapid growth in industry did not bring prosperity for all. Among the significant social problems were long hours of work for low pay, death and accidents in the mines and factories, and poor and overcrowded housing in the industrial communities. Coalmining, particularly, was a hard and dirty job, and the grim appearance of the pits showed it. It is difficult to imagine today the huge heaps of pit waste, often burning and smoking for years; or the further despoliation of the landscape by a maze of railway lines and embankments, by the quarries gouged in hillsides, and by the pollution in the streams.

157. (left) This disused quarry near
Cowshill is now a place of beauty.

Certain Durham mining villages did manage to retain more than a trace of their rural beginnings - Trimdon with its long green and Norman church, Easington with its prominent Early English church also standing high above the green. However in some other communities, there was far less to inspire the inhabitants. The workers' houses built by coal owners had not been designed for comfort or graceful living. Small and cramped, they were often laid out in long rows beside unmade streets, a mechanical and dreary environment with few diversions and facilities. Inevitably, therefore, the consequences of sustained industrial expansion brought far-reaching social changes.

The growing workforce, many of whom came into the County from elsewhere, worshipped in non-conformist chapels rather than in the established Anglican churches. They banded together to try and improve their working conditions and to get rid of such practices as eviction from colliery-owned houses during strikes. The Durham Miners' Association was formed in 1869 and the fight for rights brought forth such workers' champions as Peter Lee. It was in his memory that the new town near the coast was named.

The strength of the miners' unions was strikingly symbolised in the Annual Durham Miners' Gala when thousands of miners and their families would march into Durham City, a tradition which still attracts many visitors. A reminder of the work of the unions can also still be seen in the community institution of the 'Miners' Welfare', the heart of a mining village's existence.

In the middle of this industrial ferment and among the inventors

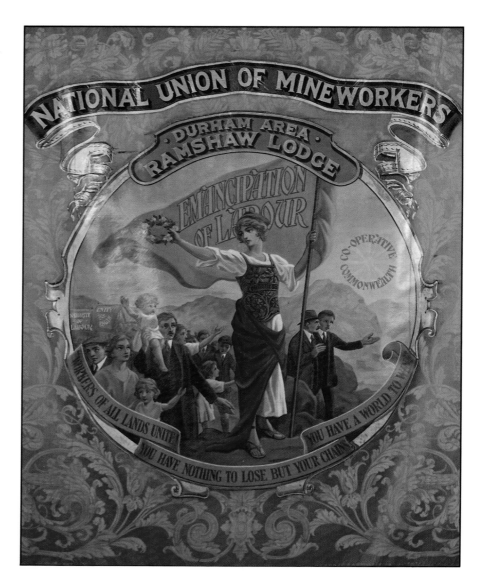

and entrepreneurs, more artistic talents were being nurtured. Thomas Sheraton, the furniture designer, lived in Stockton. William Emmerson, the mathematician, in Hurworth. Elizabeth Barrett Browning was born at Coxhoe Hall. Robert Surtees, the antiquary, lived at Mainsforth and Robert Smith Surtees, the author, at Hamsterley in the north west of the County. Lord Byron married Isabella Milbanke at Seaham and Wordsworth met his future wife at Sockburn.

The County also stimulated the talents of visitors. A house in Bowes was used by Charles Dickens as a model for Dotheboys Hall in his novel

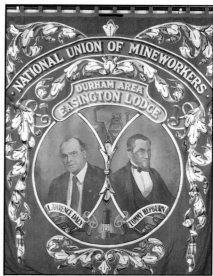

158. (top) Union banner, Ramshaw Colliery.

159. (above) Union banner, Easington Colliery.

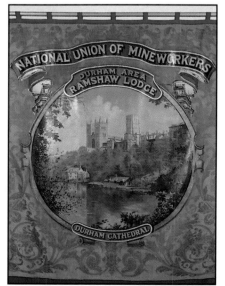

160. *(top) Union banner, Vane Tempest Colliery.*

161. *(above) Union banner, Ramshaw Colliery.*

overseas markets for coal during the Great War of 1914-18 both heralded decline. Indeed, many of the seams in the west of the County, where coal had been mined for centuries, were worked out.

Having led the Industrial Revolution, the north east now saw itself steadily overtaken. Both in Britain and abroad, its competitors invested in the latest machinery and techniques - and the world's markets noticed. In the slump in international trade during the 1920s and 1930s, unemployment in County Durham and north east England soared. When four out of every five men in Jarrow found themselves without work, the unemployed marched to London in 1936.

In those economically very difficult years, not enough was done to tackle the other Victorian legacies - poor housing and the hideous industrial landscape. Despite a return to full employment during World War II, the inherent problems of the County's economy remained and had to be tackled as a matter of urgency. In the years since the War, therefore, the rationalisation has been widespread, if not breathtaking. In excess of 80 pits have gone. The famous locomotive engineering works at Darlington have gone. The last major steel works - at Consett - has also gone.

Yet the pride and the memories remain. It is perhaps most fitting that, at the time of writing, the names of the two collieries still working - Easington Colliery and Vane Tempest - have long been associated with County Durham. Each is a worthy custodian of an outstanding tradition of innovation, achievement and reliability, a tradition which is admirably suited to a new and exciting era.

Nicholas Nickleby. Both Sir Walter Scott and the artist Turner were inspired by Teesdale - as the poem Rokeby and the painting 'Meeting of the Waters of the River Tees and Greta' respectively attest. More local and less well-known, but still works of art in their own right, are the beautiful quilts embroidered by miners' wives and now seen in the Beamish and Bowes Museums.

The immense industrial energy of the Victorians, the tenfold growth in population and the reliance on only a few heavy basic industries contained the seeds of the County's later economic difficulties. The advent of oil-fired ships and the loss of

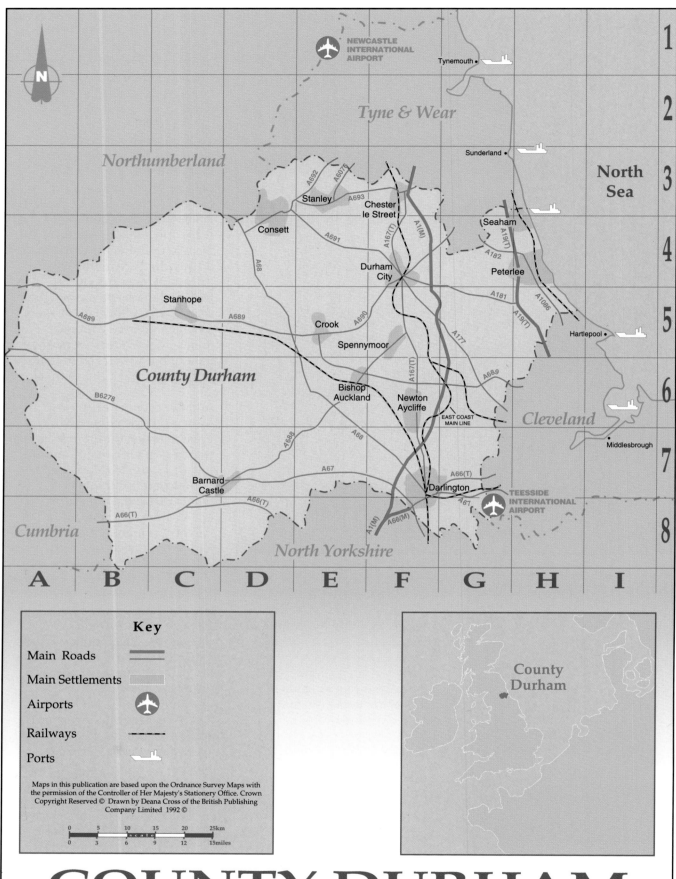

Maps in this publication are based upon the Ordnance Survey Maps with the permission of the Controller of Her Majesty's Stationery Office. Crown Copyright Reserved © Drawn by Deana Cross of the British Publishing Company Limited 1992 ©

Key

Main Roads

Main Settlements

Airports

Railways

Ports

COUNTY DURHAM
Communications

162. (above) Communication and population map.

Working in the County today

163. (above) Seaham North Harbour retains its character as a small fishing port, while the South Harbour is modern and industrial.

Lying at the centre of the North East Region, County Durham provides an outstanding strategic business location for both the UK domestic market and opportunities in continental Europe. Those appraising the County will quickly realise, however, that it offers much more. Modern, well-designed industrial facilities have been carefully integrated within the precious environment. Communications are excellent. The workforce is skilled, the young well-educated.

Approximately 592,000 people live in County Durham, mostly in small towns and villages spread throughout the County. The overall density is 2. 43 persons per hectare which compares favourably with the 3. 34 average for England and Wales.

There are 12 main towns in the County. Most have less than 30,000 inhabitants, only Durham City and Darlington have more. In the north, perched on high ground is Consett. Nearby, on another slope, lies Stanley while lower down, on the banks of the Wear, is Chester le Street. All these places have easy access to the urban areas of Tyne & Wear - Gateshead itself can be clearly seen in the distance.

Also close to Tyne & Wear are County Durham's port of Seaham and the coastal community of Peterlee.

Inland, towards the heart of the County, is Durham City itself with a population in excess of 38,000. The established towns here also include Bishop Auckland, Spennymoor and Crook.

In the south lies Newton Aycliffe and also Darlington with 85,000 residents, the largest population anywhere in the County. Further inland, in lower Teesdale, lies the market town of Barnard Castle.

It is evident that most of today's centres of population still lie north-south along the historical lines of communication. Just as these are now supported by the best road and rail services, so the infrastructure elsewhere in the County has been updated and linked into these main through-routes. Any company viewing County Durham as a prospective location in which to develop its business will indeed find a first-rate transport and communications network: the bulk of inland freight deliveries from the County's industrial sites can be made within 24 hours; deliveries by sea reach the Scandinavian and north European coasts in a similar timescale.

Supporting air travel for County Durham's industries, residents and visitors, is also impressive. There are worldwide connections from Newcastle Airport north of the boundary with Tyne & Wear, and from Teesside Airport near Darlington in the south of the County. It usually takes no more than 30 minutes to drive from Durham City to either of these airports - and a mere 10 minutes to reach Teesside from Darlington. It is with real confidence, therefore, that County Durham anticipates an especially thriving future, which will be further helped once the Channel Tunnel Euro-Freight Centre is established at Darlington.

164. (below) Newton Aycliffe industrial estate.

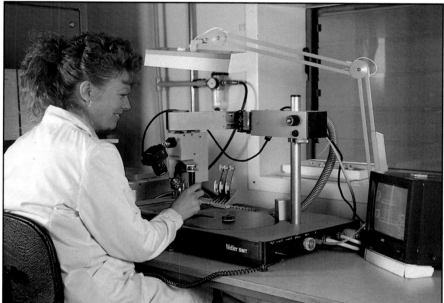

165. (top) The Fujitsu factory at Newton Aycliffe – semi conductors.

166. (centre) Integrated Micro Products, Consett – computer technology.

167. (below) ttc (UK) Ltd, Seaham – heat exchange equipment.

That working in County Durham today has a truly international flavour is convincingly demonstrated by the extent of foreign investment and trading activity. There are at least six well-known Japanese companies located within the County including Fujitsu and Sanyo (UK) Ltd, with two more just north of the boundary with Tyne & Wear which subcontract work locally. There are also 14 North American companies - among them the prominent names of Fisher Price, 3M (UK) and Coca-Cola Great Britain Ltd - and over 20 from continental Europe, including one of the largest concentrations of Scandinavian investment in Britain with companies such as ttc (UK) Ltd and Electrolux Group. There is in fact a grand total of 78 overseas companies now located on the various industrial sites. To these should be added those notable blue-chip British companies which have also recognised the benefits of County Durham as a business and manufacturing location - and those indigenous names whose reputations endure worldwide.

From the old days of coal mining, therefore, and of iron, steel and railway engineering, the County now enjoys a highly diversified and sophisticated economy. Particular strengths lie in key areas of science including electronics, information technology, engineering, advanced materials, biotechnology and pharmaceuticals. Other important areas of production are clothing, textiles, plastic processing and food and drinks. The service industries, too, are well represented.

168. (above left) 169. (below left)
Farm transport old and new:

The conventional tractor . . .

. . . A Teesdale farmer finds three
wheels are more suited to the upper
moors.

170. (above) Sheepdog trials,
Wolsingham.

171. (left) Sheep-shearing – the
traditional way.

Prominent in the rural economy are those small concerns which can be found inland and up in the Dales as craft or cottage industries, so often associated with the many farms and small holdings. Yet industrial production is by no means restricted to the eastern half of the County. That Wear Valley and Teesdale also lie mostly within an Area of Outstanding Natural Beauty brings credit upon the husbandry and care of all who live and work there.

Undoubtedly one of the County's greatest assets is its people. New companies attracted to the area have consistently been well pleased with their experience of the local workforce - its skills, loyalty and adaptability. The low labour turnover and rates of absenteeism are regarded as extremely favourable.

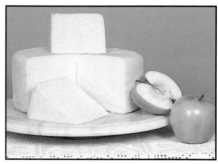

172. (far left) The technique of dry stone walling.

173. (top left) Classical creamware from Newton Aycliffe.

174. (left) Cheesemaking at The North of England Open Air Museum, Beamish.

175. (above) Cotherstone cheese from Teesdale – a traditional, golden, creamy cheese with piquant taste.

In industrial relations, too, County Durham enjoys a good reputation: the vast majority of companies in recent years has neither experienced any serious official disputes nor been subjected to unofficial strikes of any consequence. It is also worth noting the experience of the Black & Decker plant at Spennymoor: since it was established in the late 1960s, this manufacturer has enjoyed a dispute-free record.

The preparedness of the labour force to be flexible in its approach to work patterns has undoubtedly made a singular contribution to the County's achievements in productivity and industrial relations. Differing shift-work permutations, for example, some distinctly continental in origin, have become established practice throughout County Durham for both men and women.

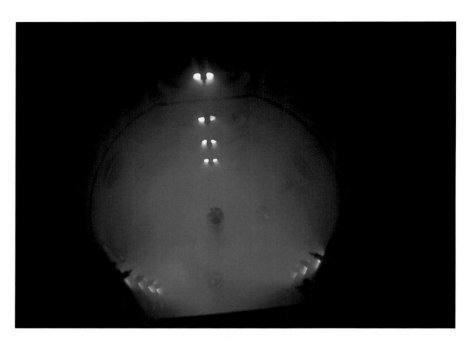

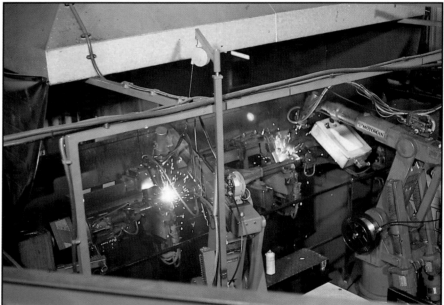

176. (top right) Machine tool coating in Consett.

177. (centre right) Robotic welding in Newton Aycliffe.

178. (right) South Durham Training Centre, Newton Aycliffe.

179. (far right) Milburngate Shopping Centre.

180. (bottom far right) The Palace Green University Library, Durham City.

Education, too, is transforming remarkably the potential of those who work here today and of those who will join the economy tomorrow. The County has a good mix of modern, well equipped and well staffed nursery, primary and secondary schools. There is a wide range of mainstream and specialist school provision, together with support services for children with special needs.

Also located widely across the County are six Colleges of Further Education which provide academic and vocational courses on a part and full-time basis. These include a College of Agriculture on the outskirts of Durham City and additionally there is a Residential College for Adult Education at Beamish. There are outdoor activity centres, music centres, an environmental education centre and flourishing activities in the many sports facilities. Undoubtedly, the men and women of County Durham are fitter, healthier, better educated and better trained than at any other time.

Durham University dates back to 1832 when the traditional powers of the Prince Bishops were formally disolved, and the Bishop and the Dean and Chapter gave property for the foundation of Durham University. This collegiate University with its fourteen colleges and many attractive buildings is the third oldest in England. Its work covers key branches of science and technology and traditional areas of scholarship. Durham graduates are in great demand amongst employers and the University helps to attract investment into the County. The current Chancellor and formal Head of the University is the celebrated actor and writer Sir Peter Ustinov.

The task of guiding, shaping and promoting the County's changing potential during decades of radical social and economic transformation has posed formidable challenges for local government. By careful management of its development plans, however, the County has implemented a number of important initiatives. These underpin the improving economic health of the County, the maintenance of its outstanding environment and the substantial enhancement of individual skill levels. By careful investment and support for business, fresh opportunities are being created and new expectations fulfilled. The economy is becoming progressively more robust, diverse and self-sustaining in order to meet the needs and aspirations of the people.

The County has indeed come a long way from the days when consumptive boys smashed lead ore with crude iron hammers. Or when the red pollution from steel-making in Consett could be seen for miles around.

Leisure

181. (left) Country life at Beamish.

182. (above) Causey Arch.

A more sophisticated economy and the growth of leisure opportunities have raised the expectations of the population of County Durham. The range of activities available to both residents and visitors has increased in turn - but so, too, have concern and regard for the County's rich heritage. This has been cleverly preserved and stunningly displayed at a number of immensely popular locations.

The North of England Open Air Museum at Beamish is famous beyond County Durham. In an attractive rural setting of more than 200 acres, today's generations can experience, and even sometimes remind themselves of, the quality of life in the north east before the Great War of 1914-18. The invitation to touch, taste and experiment provides a wonderfully vivid journey back in time. Its vigorous approach to the past and its efforts to extend the displays have earned Beamish both European and British Museum of the Year Awards.

Curiosity and imagination are similarly stimulated at the Lead Mining Centre at Killhope. Children, particularly, respond with fascination to the opportunity of trying the process out for themselves. Indeed, education in its most enjoyable form is a speciality of County Durham. At Causey Arch, for example, the oldest surviving railway arch in the world can be marvelled at while exploring the wooded gorge and waggonways. At Darlington's Railway Centre and Museum, and again at those Shildon Works of Timothy Hackworth, the locomotives of yesterday are there to be examined and discussed. The enthusiast can even link all these experiences - by testing the rolling stock on The Heritage Line to Stanhope or on the Tanfield Railway at Causey.

COACH to REDCAR,

IN CONNECTION WITH THE

Great North of England, and Stockton and Darlington Railways.

A NEAT   LIGHT

FOUR INSIDE   **FAST COACH,**

CALLED THE

OCEAN

LEAVES

THE STOCKTON AND DARLINGTON RAILWAY STATION,

STOCKTON,

ON THE ARRIVAL OF THE

TRAIN FROM MANCHESTER, LEEDS, AND YORK.

Leaves York at 11·30 ; Thirsk, 12·33 ; Northallerton, 12·56 ; Darlington, 2·30.

Passengers Booked from Thirsk and Northallerton Railway Stations

TO REDCAR.

The OCEAN COACH leaves REDCAR at 9 o'Clock in the Morning, in time for the Great North of England Railway Train, which leaves Darlington at a quarter-past 12.

June 23, 1842.

J. READMAN, PRINTER, DARLINGTON.

The process of restoring and revealing County Durham's past achievements continues widely. At the Tees Cottage Pumping Station in Darlington, for example, the former Darlington Waterworks are being developed as a waterworks museum. There is also a heritage centre in Durham City. At Stanhope in Weardale, the Durham Dales Centre is a pleasant, burgeoning focus for traditional crafts and industries. The list can only grow as diverse communities in this County of contrasts come to realise that the commonplace for them can be a source of valid interest to the visitor and enquirer.

183. (top far left) Tanfield Railway, one of the oldest existing railways in the world, started life in 1725 as a wooden waggonway powered by horses.

184. (bottom far left) The Timothy Hackworth Victorian Railway Museum, Shildon.

185. (left) Travel poster dating from 1842.

186. The Darlington Railway Centre and Museum.

187. (left) The Weardale Museum, Ireshopeburn, vividly portrays cottage life towards the end of the Victorian era – the building itself has links with John Wesley who preached in the adjoining chapel.

188. (above) Town life, The North of England Open Air Museum, Beamish.

189. (below) The 'washing floor' at Killhope – young people experience the rigorous work of yesterday's lead mining industry.

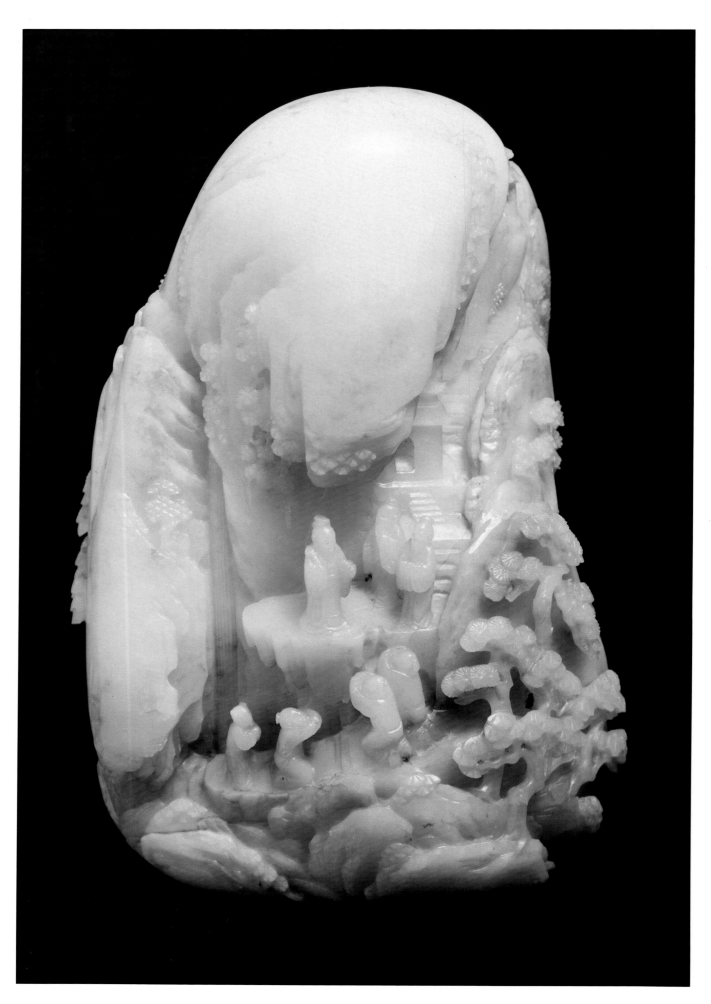

Excellence and rarity extend to County Durham's more formal museums. Fine art and the relics of religious and ancient history abound. Masterpieces and artefacts are displayed in sometimes breathtaking surroundings.

A short stroll from the centre of Barnard Castle in Teesdale is the remarkable Bowes Museum built in County Durham between 1860 and 1892 when it was first opened to the public. The museum contains the outstanding international art collection of industrialist, MP and aristocrat, John Bowes, and of his Parisian-born actress wife, Josephine. What an appropriate and enlightening legacy his wealth and her inspiration have left the cultural life and architectural tradition of the County.

In Durham, a unique collection of sculptures, paintings and porcelain from Japan, China, Tibet and Egypt is exhibited in the Oriental Museum, Durham University.

190. (far left) An 18th Century Jade Mountain from the Oriental Museum, Durham University, shows a Chinese shrine with three gods being worshipped by a group of pilgrims.

191. (top left) The Bowes Museum illuminated.

192. (left) The tears of St Peter by Domenikos Theotocopoulos – a fine example of El Greco's work exhibited in the Bowes Museum.

Also part of the University is the impressive Museum of Archaeology at The Old Fulling Mill on the banks of the Wear. The Museum illustrates the history of the City but includes material of international importance from other locations, too.

No less significant is local art which is encouraged throughout the County. Some compelling examples exist. Near Prebends' Bridge, for example, by the river below Durham Cathedral, there is a remarkable carving on tree trunks showing the detail of the Last Supper - entitled 'The Upper Room'. On the walls of the Durham Dales Centre, murals by residents and school pupils depict the life and history of the Dales. The Durham City and Darlington Art Galleries, too, have done much for artists in the area. Darlington's Museum has successfully blended local social and natural history. The performing arts have blossomed as well - in Darlington, in Peterlee and in Durham City. Jazz, folk and the brass band tradition flourish as much as classical music. The excellent Durham Art Gallery has done much to promote them all.

In a somewhat quieter vein are the many unguessed mysteries of Durham Cathedral. The Treasury and Monks' Dormitory contain relics of St Cuthbert, some magnificent silver plate and beautiful illuminated manuscripts. The pillars, vaults and stained glass windows are works of art, too. More modest but just as precious are the features and adornments of the County's many fascinating parish churches. For example, the rich arcades and wall painting of St Lawrence's at Pittington, the unspoilt 12th Century interior of St Helen's at St Helen's Auckland, and the 7th Century Saxon Church at Escomb, near Bishop Auckland.

Memorabilia of different religious persuasions can also be found in the County. At the Ankers House Museum in Chester le Street, there is an intimate display of Ankerite history and beliefs - while, at Ireshopeburn, the origins of John Wesley's Methodism are most interestingly revealed.

193. *(top left) In the Market Place, Durham City, stands a statue of the third Marquess of Londonderry, the famous soldier and politician who founded Seaham harbour for the export of coal.*

194. *(bottom left) St Mary's Church, Trimdon.*

195. *(above) St Brandon's Church, Brancepeth.*

196. *(left) The Ankers House Museum, Chester le Street, gives an insight into the retreat of an Ankerite or Ankeress – walled up for life passing the time in prayer and contemplation.*

197. (above) Riverbank art – Colin Wilbourne's exceptional work, 'The Upper Room', stands besides Prebends' Bridge in Durham City.

198. (right) The Durham Light Infantry Museum building incorporates The Durham Art Gallery as well as preserving the history of the 'Faithfuls'.

199. (top right) In the 14th Century, the Chapel of the hospital of St Mary Magdalene, Durham City, served the inmates of the hospital administered by the Almoner of the Priory of Durham.

200. (bottom right) The Saxon-Norman Church of St Lawrence at Pittington has been described as 'the Mother Church of Durham' – there has been a settlement on the site since earliest times.

The evidence of yesterday's invasions and power struggles is plentiful and waiting to be explored. At Piercebridge on the north bank of the River Tees near Darlington, the village is built almost entirely within the site of the Roman fort. The unnatural land formation around the village reveals the ancient perimeter. At Binchester Roman Fort near Bishop Auckland, the house of the fort commander includes the best example of a Roman military bath suite in Britain. At Bowes Castle, too, Roman foundations underpin the old stone keep.

For further excursions into early history and the Middle Ages, however, there is no better starting point than the home of the Prince Bishops itself. Durham Castle is, in layout and in detail, one of the best preserved Norman strongholds in the country. The atmosphere is intoxicating and one's appetite for yet more scenes of history grows. Try Barnard Castle, Raby Castle, Finchale Priory and Egglestone Abbey. Or for later beauty, Auckland Castle and Rokeby Park.

201. (above) Raby Castle Gardens.

202. (below) Durham Castle seen from Elvet Bridge.

203. (right) The Town Hall, Durham City, was opened in 1851 – on its walls are displayed the arms of the City Guilds which played such an important part in civic life from the 14th to the 19th Century.

Exciting and provocative though these fabulous sites of history and literature may be, there is scarcely any better way of invigorating the mind and body than to wander in the County's beautiful countryside. There is a remarkable choice of scenery to complement the more familiar dales and moors, the waterfalls and Pennine Way. Converted railway lines, for example, now offer excellent views and comfortable walking. Hamsterley Forest, too, is delightful for its peace, shade, paths and streams - while close to Darlington is a glorious walk along the banks of the River Tees, and only minutes from the centre of Durham City is deep woodland along the River Wear. The coast and its denes should not be overlooked either. The sand is golden at Seaham and Crimdon and the seaward views from Beacon Hill are marvellous in the early morning light.

There has been much work throughout the County in developing country parks and picnic areas in ways that will

204. (above) Houghall Woods, Durham City.

205. (below) Red squirrels can still be seen in County Durham's woodlands.

206. (right) The garden at Leap Mill Farm, Burnopfield – the farm has the best preserved 18th Century watermill in County Durham.

appeal to families. Many of these are sensibly adjacent to the better-known sites like Beamish and the Derwent and Lanchester Valley Walks. However some have become attractions in their own right - Low Barnes near Witton le Wear with its nature reserve and visitor centre; the lake and nature trails of Hardwick Hall Country Park; the lowland heath of Waldridge Fell; and the pretty beck at Bowlees.

207. (right) Eggleston Hall Gardens – colourful and attractive whatever the season.

208. (below) Gibson's Cave, Bowlees.

209. (far right) Bowlees picnic area, Teesdale.

210. *(above) Beacon Hill, County Durham coast – at one time fires were lit here on the highest point on Durham's coastline to warn sailors of the treacherous reefs below.*

212. *(right) The Waskerley Way – one of County Durham's best known railway walks.*

211. *(below) The Fearon Walk, Durham City, from Elvet Bridge to Kingsgate Bridge.*

Sport, too, has become increasingly important to the health and vitality of County Durham. The strong, traditional pastimes remain as the annual shows in Weardale and Teesdale demonstrate. Even the Sedgefield ball game continues unchanged after more than 900 years. To such locally significant events as racing at Sedgefield and rowing in the historic Durham Regatta can now be added new achievements. Fishing, golf, watersports and equestrianism all flourish. The annual County Durham International Cross Country Races are now an established date in the athletics calendar and form part of the IAAF World Cross Country Challenge Grand Prix. They attract many athletes of world class renown. Proudest of all in its newly won first-class colours of 1992, is the Durham County Cricket Club itself. The Club does not yet have its own ground but, within a season or two, will occupy a permanent home at the Riverside Ground below Lumley Castle in Chester le Street.

213. (above left) Waldridge Fell, County Durham – the County's best surviving lowland heath provides a natural habitat for many wild flowers.

215. (above) Fly fishing on the River Wear.

214. (below left) The River Tees near Sockburn – it is possible that, at this ford, the Bishop received the Falchion from the Lord of the Manor.

216. (below) Golf at Brancepeth Castle.

217. (above) Canoeists at Low Force, Teesdale.

218. (below) First Class Cricket at the University Ground, Durham City.

219. (right) A rowing four at Elvet Bridge.

220. *(left) The International Cross Country Race, December 1991 – Britain's Liz McColgan is front on the left.*

221. *(below left) Ice Hockey – the Durham Wasps in action.*

222. *(right) Old time music hall – entertainment for any taste.*

223. *(below) Spennymoor Leisure Centre.*

224. (left) 'The Prince Bishop' pleasure cruiser.

225. (above) Street artists in Durham Market Place.

County Durham

Land of the Prince Bishops

Undoubtedly, this is a high quality and splendidly healthy place in which to live, work and bring up a family. There is both a richness and a diversity about life and leisure in County Durham. Richness because nothing is done without complete commitment, and diversity because there is so much to be done. Whatever one's inclinations - solitude, people, entertainment, activity - there is a wealth of each waiting to be discovered.

The Future

226a & b. (left) The Prince Bishops' Garden from the 1990 Garden Festival has now been reconstructed at the University Botanic Garden in Durham City.

227. (above) Meeting of the social affairs, Employment and the Working Environment commitee of the European Parliament, which held its 'out of Brussels' meeting at County Hall from 30th May to 1st June 1990.

County Durham rightly views the future with optimism. After fifty years spent disengaging the economy from the confining effects of two centuries of extraordinary, world-beating industrialisation, the process of restructuring is now advancing in a controlled way. The challenge has undoubtedly been greatest in the former coalmining communities, the single pivot of the County's earlier wealth. By careful planning and coordination, an effective transition is being made to a balanced economic structure as the last of the collieries close.

There is much to anticipate: the continuing development of new industries and traditional skills; the possibilities presented to the County by the Visual Arts Year in 1996; new environmental achievements; new sporting victories.

Links with continental Europe and an appetite for international business are also at the forefront of the County's consciousness. Notable liaisons have been formed with the Departement of the Somme in France, with Kreis Wesel and Tubingen in Germany, Banska Bystrica in Slovakia, Kostroma in Russia and Nakskov in Denmark. More will undoubtedly follow.

Those who live and work in County Durham today should be confident of their ability to develop these liaisons, to attract new partners and to exploit fresh opportunities. For theirs is a County with a history and tradition second to none. They hail from a lovely stretch of English countryside and have forebears who were strong, independent and imaginitive.

Those values will stand them in excellent stead tomorrow.

Acknowledgements

The County Council would like to thank the Director of Economic Development, Ken Frankish and his staff, Harry Elliott, Geoff Hughes and Karen Harris, for their very considerable assistance in the preparation of the book, Ian Stewart and all others who provided advice, information, comments and photographs. Philip Nixon has also provided supporting material and most photographs apart from those listed below.

John Beatty	171
John Burles	220, 221
Stan Gamester	158, 159, 160, 161
Darlington Borough Council	152
A.P.S. (UK) Richmond	75
Oriental Museum, Durham University	190
The Bowes Museum	192
North News and Pictures, Newcastle upon Tyne	218

Line illustrations by: Mike Hein-Hartmann

Cover design by: Andy Tibbs

Maps by: Deana Cross

Further Reading

ADEY, T.	County Durham through the ages. 1990.
ALLSOP, B.ed.	Modern architecture of Northern England. 1969.
ATKINSON, F.	Life and tradition in Northumberland and Durham. 1986.
ATKINSON, F.	Industrial archaeology of North East England. 2 Vols. 1974.
AYER, T.T.	Annfield Plain in old picture postcards. 2nd ed. 1990.
BELL, W.	The road to Jericho: (life in the Durham coalfield.) 1980.
BILLINGS, R.W.	Illustrations of the architectural antiquities of the County of Durham. Facsimile reprint. 1974.
BLAIR, P.H.	Northumbria in the days of Bede. 1976.
BOWES, P.	Weardale: clearing the forest. 1990.
BULMER, M.ed.	Mining and social change: Durham County in the twentieth century. 1978.
	Castles of County Durham (six reproduction prints). 1979.
CLACK, P.A.G.	Archaeology in the North. 1976.
CLAPHAM, A.R.	Upper Teesdale: the area and its natural history. 1978.
COGGINS, D.	Teesdale in old photographs. 1989.
COIA, A.J.	Spennymoor in old picture postcards. 2nd ed. 1988.
CROSBY, J.ed.	Durham in old photographs. 1990.
CROSBY, J.H.	Ignatius Bonomi of Durham, Architect. 1987.
CROSBY, J.	Weardale in old photographs. 1989.
	Darlington (six reproduction prints). 1975.
	Durham City (six reproduction prints). 1975.
DURHAM COUNTY COUNCIL	Lead and life at Killhope. 1987.
EAST DURHAM COMMUNITY ARTS	East Durham heritage trails and walkways. 1988.
FLYNN, G.	Darlington in old photographs. 1989.

FORDYCE, W.	A history of coal, coke and coalfields . . . iron, its ores and process of manufacture. 1973. (Facsimile reprint of 1860 ed.)
FYNES, R.	The miners of Northumberland and Durham: a history of their social and political progress. 1986. (First publ. 1873).
GARSIDE, W.R.	The Durham Miners, 1919-1960. 1971.
GIBBY, C.W.	A short history of Durham City. 3rd ed. 1975.
GOODHART, J.S.	Weardale: valley of the Prince Bishops. 1988.
GRAHAM, G.G.	The flora and vegetation of County Durham. 1988.
HAIR, T.H.	Sketches of the coalmines in Northumberland and Durham. 1969. (Facsimile reprint of 1844 ed.)
HAMILTON, R.	Palatine pathways: walking the history of Durham's Prince Bishops. 1988.
HINDHAUGH, R.	Stanley in old picture postcards. 2nd ed. 1990.
INSTITUTE OF GEOLOGICAL SCIENCES	Geology of the country around Barnard Castle: exploration of one-inch geological sheet, 32. (New series). 1976.
INSTITUTE OF GEOLOGICAL SCIENCES	Geology of the country between Durham and West Hartlepool: exploration of one-inch geological sheet, 27 (New series). 1967.
JOHNSON, M.	Durham: historic and university city. 4th ed. 1983.
KEARNEY, T.	Painted red: a social history of Consett, 1840-1990. 1990.
MCCORD, N.	North East England: the region's development 1760-1960. 1979.
MCDOUGALL, C.A.	The Stockton and Darlington Railway, 1821-1863. 2nd ed. 1975.
MARCHBANK, B.	Durham quilting. 1988.
MARCOMBE, D.ed.	The last principality: politics, religion and society in the Bishopric of Durham, 1494-1660. 1987.
MOORE, R.	Pitmen, preachers and politics: the effects of Methodism in a Durham Mining Community. 1974.
MORRIS, R.J.B.	The city of Durham: its town hall, guildhall and civic traditions. 1984.
MOYES, W.A.	The banner book: a study of the banners of the lodges of Durham Miners' Association. 1974.
NELSON, I.	Bygone County Durham. 1990.
NELSON, I.	Durham as it was. 1974.
PEVSNER, N.	County Durham. 2nd ed. 1983. (Reprint 1953 edition.) (The Buildings of England.)
POCOCK, D.C.D.	Durham: portrait of a cathedral city. 1983.
POCOCK, D.C.D.	Durham: images of a cathedral city. 1975.
POCOCK, D.C.D.	A history of County Durham. 1990.
PROUD, K.	The Prince Bishops of Durham: from early times to the dissolution of the monasteries 995 - 1539 AD. 1990.
RAISTRICK, A.	The life and work of the Northern lead miner. 1990.
ROBERTS, B.K.	The green villages of County Durham. 1977.
SHEA, W.	Carpet making in Durham City. 1984.
SIMPSON, D.A.	Prince Bishop country: the people, history and folklore of Co. Durham and the River Wear. 1991.
TEGNER, H.S.	Natural history in Northumberland and Durham. 1972.
THOMAS, D. St.J. & C.R. Clinker eds.	A regional history of the railways of Great Britain. Vol.4. North East England by K. Hoole. 3rd ed. 1986.
THOROLD, H.	County Durham. 1980.
TOMLINSON, W.W.	The North Eastern Railway: its rise and development. 2nd ed. 1967.
TURNBULL, L.	The history of lead mining in the North East of England. 1975.
WALKER. T.E.C.	Durham: twixt Tyne and Tees. 1990. (Reprint 1953 ed.)
WHITE, P.A.	Portrait of County Durham. 2nd ed. 1976.
WHITTAKER, N.	Historic architecture of County Durham. 1971.
WHITTAKER, N.	The old halls and manor houses of Durham. 1975.
WILCOCK, D.	The Durham coalfield. Part 1. The 'sea coal' age. 1979.
WILKINSON, A.	Barnard Castle in old picture postcards. Vol.1. 4th ed. 1990. Vol.2. 1990.
WOOD, C.F.	Bishop Auckland in old picture postcards. 1985.

MAPS

The following five sheets provide a coverage of the whole County in the Ordnance Survey LANDRANGER SERIES at a scale of 1:50 000:–

Sheet Number	Title
87	Hexham, Haltwhistle and surrounding area
88	Tyneside and Durham area
91	Appleby in Westmorland area
92	Barnard Castle and surrounding area
93	Middlesbrough and Darlington area